DETECTING DISASTERS
DETECTING AVALANCHES

by Trudi Strain Trueit

FOCUS READERS

WWW.NORTHSTAREDITIONS.COM

Produced for North Star Editions by Red Line Editorial.

Photographs ©: Lysogor Roman/Shutterstock Images, cover, 1; Lee Chamberlin/Shutterstock Images, 4–5; Rapho Agence/Science Source, 7; marima-design/iStockphoto, 8–9; Kevin Davidson/iStockphoto, 11; Travers Eric/Sipa/AP Images, 13; Smith Collection/Gado/Getty Images, 14–15; Patrick Gardin/AP Images, 16; Ashley Smith/Times-News/AP Images, 18; National Weather Service, 20–21; mato/Shutterstock Images, 22–23; Patrick Landmann/Science Source, 25; Matthias Schrader/AP Images, 27; Rick Bowmer/AP Images, 28

Content Consultant: Jordy Hendrikx, Associate Professor of Geography, Snow and Avalanche Lab, Department of Earth Sciences, Montana State University

ISBN
978-1-63517-000-9 (hardcover)
978-1-63517-056-6 (paperback)
978-1-63517-162-4 (ebook pdf)
978-1-63517-112-9 (hosted ebook)

Library of Congress Control Number: 2016950114

Printed in the United States of America
Mankato, MN
November, 2016

ABOUT THE AUTHOR

A former television weather forecaster, Trudi Strain Trueit has written more than 100 fiction and nonfiction books for children. Born and raised in the Pacific Northwest, she enjoys hiking and photography (often both at the same time).

TABLE OF CONTENTS

CHAPTER 1

WHITE DEATH

In February 2012, a group of 16 expert skiers gathered at Stevens Pass ski resort in Washington State. Nearly 3 feet (0.9 m) of snow had fallen on the mountains in the past three days. The skiers planned to ski an area called Tunnel Creek. It was risky. At first everything seemed fine.

The Stevens Pass area in Washington State has a history of dangerous avalanches.

Suddenly, a crack appeared in the snow. A huge slab of snow broke away from the hillside. It was an avalanche! The slide snapped trees and ripped off their bark. Three of the skiers were killed.

As more people venture into risky areas, the death toll from avalanches

A SURVIVOR'S STORY

Professional skier Elyse Saugstad was swept downhill in the Tunnel Creek avalanche. She compared the experience to being in a washing machine. Tossed wildly, she was not sure she would make it. Saugstad survived thanks to an **air bag backpack**. This device inflated and kept her only partially buried. Rescuers soon found her.

An avalanche can be deadly to people on a mountain's slopes.

rises. Approximately 120 people die in avalanches every year, 30 of them in the United States. The popularity of outdoor winter sports has made understanding avalanches more critical than ever.

CHAPTER 2

SIGNS OF TROUBLE

Every mountain snowfall adds another layer to the winter **snowpack**. Each layer of snow has its own characteristics, such as texture, strength, and types of snow crystals. The weakest layer in the snowpack can spell trouble. Too much weight on top of it may cause it to break. Sometimes just one skier can do it.

Snowfall in the mountains creates beautiful landscapes, but it can also lead to avalanches.

The slab slides downhill, taking all the snow above it and picking up more on the way. An avalanche may weigh millions of pounds and travel as fast as a car on the freeway.

Avalanches almost always come with warning signs. People can learn to recognize these signs. A rapid rise in air temperatures is one such clue. This quick warming will melt snow, weakening the snowpack. Another concern is a storm that dumps several feet of new snow. This adds weight to the snowpack, increasing the avalanche threat. Snow already on the ground may pose a risk, too. Winds can move snow to other slopes and shape it

Areas with high avalanche risk may have road signs warning people of the possible danger.

into dangerous positions. A cornice is an overhang of snow on a ridge. Winds push snow into this position. A cornice can easily break off and trigger a slide.

Detecting avalanche warning signs and alerting the public to danger are the duties of avalanche forecasters.

These experts post an avalanche advisory for their region each day from winter through early spring. Avalanche danger is ranked as low, considerable, high, or extreme. When the danger is rated high or extreme, avalanches are very likely to happen. Ski resorts and road crews check the stability in their own areas. They may

SNOW DETECTIVES

Avalanche forecasters typically have a degree in Earth sciences or engineering. They may work for a ski resort, an outdoor adventure company, a highway department, their state, or an avalanche center. Most of the 20 avalanche centers across the United States are operated by the US Forest Service.

Workers set up explosives to cause a controlled avalanche.

use explosive charges to bring down the hazardous masses of snow. Outdoor sports enthusiasts depend on local **advisories** to make safe decisions in the backcountry.

CHAPTER 3

WEATHER WATCH

Nothing affects avalanche danger more than the weather. Snowfall and wind are responsible for creating and shaping the snowpack. Avalanche forecasters keep close watch on the skies because weather conditions in the mountains can change quickly.

A forecaster checks a weather monitoring station in a mountainous area of Montana.

People traveling in snowy, mountainous areas must pay close attention to weather forecasts.

Forecasters may take manual weather observations. Their instruments include a thermometer to measure snow and air temperatures, an **anemometer** to detect wind speed, and a vane to show the wind direction. A snow sampling tube is used to gauge snow depth and density.

Most avalanche centers gather data from automated weather stations. The stations are placed on mountains. They measure temperature, wind speed and direction, **precipitation**, humidity, snow depth, and **solar radiation**. The stations regularly send data to computers at the nearest avalanche center.

The US Department of Agriculture runs a network of weather stations called SNOTEL. More than 800 of these stations collect information about snow and send it to scientists.

Workers test snow depth at a SNOTEL station in Idaho.

Avalanche forecasters also receive regular weather forecasts and **satellite** images from the National Weather

Service. Satellites in space observe developing storms and track their movements. The images these satellites produce allow scientists to estimate snow cover and snowfall accumulations.

Another weather tool avalanche forecasters rely on is Doppler radar. This technology measures motion within a storm. Doppler radar can detect wind speeds, as well as the type and intensity of precipitation. It can gauge how far away the storm is and how fast it is moving. The National Weather Service operates a network of 160 Doppler radar sites across the United States.

DOPPLER RADAR

These images collected by US weather radar show a massive snowstorm that hit the Midwest on December 11, 2010.

9:15 a.m.

1:15 p.m.

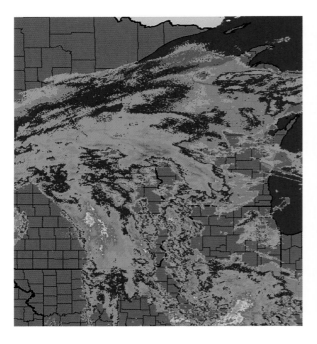

The red and yellow areas show the heaviest precipitation. The radar lets meteorologists track how storms change over time.

5:15 p.m.

9:15 p.m.

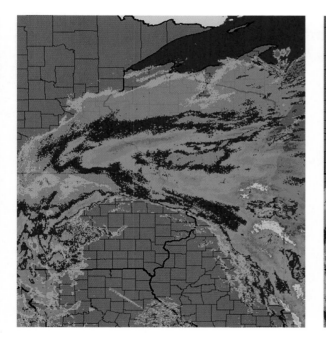

CHAPTER 4

IN THE SLIDE ZONE

Many forecasters travel to mountains to examine the **terrain** and snowpack. They take safety equipment and a partner. Avalanches tend to occur on slopes steeper than 30 degrees, so an **inclinometer** is used to measure the angle of a hill. Forecasters also note the placement of trees, bushes, and rocks.

People use helicopters to study avalanche areas and carry out rescues.

23

These objects act as anchors to help hold snow in place. However, they may also become dangerous in an avalanche. Nearly one-quarter of avalanche victims in the United States die from hitting trees and other objects as they are swept downhill.

In the field, forecasters perform various snow stability tests to detect weak layers. One method is called a compression test. A forecaster digs a snow pit, leaving a column of snow. He or she places a shovel face down on top of the column. Then the forecaster begins tapping the shovel, completing three sets of ten taps. Each set is harder than the one before it.

Some scientists simulate avalanches in their laboratories to learn how they work.

Observing when the snow drops, breaks, or pops reveals how weak the layer of snow is. A newer, similar technique called the extended column test looks at a wider area of snow. It shows a layer's weakness,

SOUNDS OF SURVIVAL

Someone buried beneath the snow has enough air to breathe for approximately 15 minutes. For this reason, an avalanche transceiver is an important tool for anyone heading into remote snowy areas. The palm-sized device can send and receive electronic signals. If a person is buried by an avalanche, his or her partners can turn on their transceivers to receive the signal. Rescue teams can then track the signal, find the person in the snow, and dig the person out.

Rescue crews sometimes use dogs to help track down people buried by avalanches.

and it provides more information about how likely a fracture is to spread.

 Air bag backpacks can help prevent people from being buried in avalanches.

In most avalanches involving deaths in the United States, the event was triggered by a person's movements. Skiers, adventurers, and explorers can learn how to recognize the signs of avalanches and use safety equipment to save many lives—including their own.

AVALANCHE SAFETY CHECKLIST

- Be aware of what areas are at risk for avalanches. Taking an avalanche course is an excellent way to know these risks.

- Check local avalanche forecasts to find out about potentially dangerous conditions.

- Always watch for factors that could trigger an avalanche, such as steep slopes or warming temperatures.

- Make sure you have the right equipment: a transceiver, a shovel, an avalanche probe, and a partner.

- If caught in an avalanche, call out for help so others know where you are.

- If you find a person buried beneath the snow, dig him or her out, starting slightly downhill. Then provide first aid and keep the person warm.

FOCUS ON
DETECTING
AVALANCHES

Write your answers on a separate piece of paper.

1. Write a sentence that describes the key ideas from Chapter 2.

2. Do you think the government should be responsible for providing avalanche forecasts to the public? Why or why not?

3. What weather condition commonly occurs before an avalanche?
- **A.** quickly warming temperatures
- **B.** quickly cooling temperatures
- **C.** temperatures that remain the same for a long time

4. Why do avalanches tend to occur on steep slopes?
- **A.** More snow falls on steep slopes.
- **B.** Temperatures are higher on steep slopes.
- **C.** The force of gravity pulls the snow down.

Answer key on page 32.

GLOSSARY

advisories
Public bulletins issued to warn of danger.

air bag backpack
An inflatable backpack designed to help prevent the wearer from being buried during an avalanche.

anemometer
An instrument for measuring wind speeds.

inclinometer
An instrument for measuring the angle of a slope.

precipitation
Water that falls from clouds to the ground in the form of rain, hail, or snow.

satellite
A spacecraft that orbits Earth, often to collect information.

snowpack
The buildup of packed snow in a mountainous region.

solar radiation
The energy given off by the sun.

terrain
The physical features of an area of land.

TO LEARN MORE

BOOKS

Hand, Carol. *The Science of an Avalanche.* Ann Arbor, MI: Cherry Lake, 2016.

Spilsbury, Richard. *The Science of Avalanches.* New York: Gareth Stevens, 2013.

Suen, Anastasia. *Avalanches.* Vero Beach, FL: Rourke Educational Media, 2016.

NOTE TO EDUCATORS

Visit **www.focusreaders.com** to find lesson plans, activities, links, and other resources related to this title.

INDEX

Answer Key: 1. Answers will vary; **2.** Answers will vary; **3.** A; **4.** C